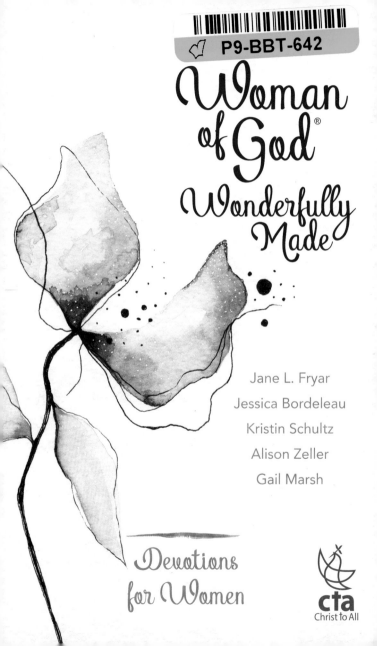

P9-BBT-642

Woman of God®
Wonderfully Made

Jane L. Fryar

Jessica Bordeleau

Kristin Schultz

Alison Zeller

Gail Marsh

Devotions
for Women

cta
Christ to All

The vision of CTA is
to see Christians highly effective
in their ministry so that Christ's Kingdom
is strengthened and expanded.

Woman of God® Wonderfully Made

Devotions for Women

Jane L. Fryar, Jessica Bordeleau, Kristin Schultz,
Alison Zeller, Gail Marsh

Copyright © 2020 CTA, Inc.
1625 Larkin Williams Rd.
Fenton, MO 63026
www.CTAinc.com

All rights reserved. No part of this publication may be reproduced, stored in a retrieval system, or transmitted, in any form or by any means, electronic, mechanical, photocopying, recording, or otherwise, without the prior written permission of CTA, Inc.

Unless otherwise indicated, Scripture quotations are taken from The Holy Bible, English Standard Version® (ESV®) Copyright © 2001 by Crossway, a publishing ministry of Good News Publishers. All rights reserved. ESV Text Edition: 2016

Scripture quotations marked NLT are taken from the Holy Bible, New Living Translation, copyright © 1996, 2004, 2015 by Tyndale House Foundation. Used by permission of Tyndale House Publishers, Inc., Carol Stream, Illinois 60188. All rights reserved.

ISBN 978-1-947699-77-9
PRINTED IN THAILAND

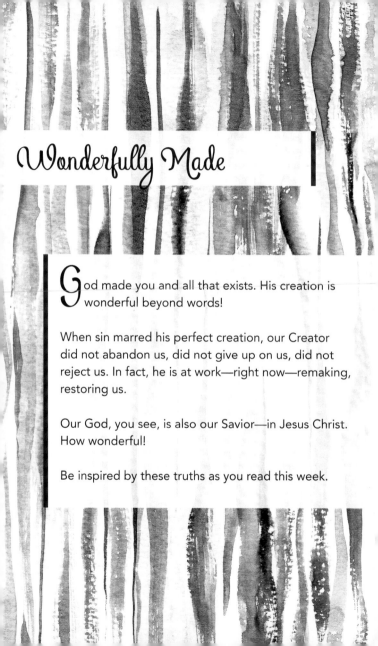

Wonderfully Made

God made you and all that exists. His creation is wonderful beyond words!

When sin marred his perfect creation, our Creator did not abandon us, did not give up on us, did not reject us. In fact, he is at work—right now—remaking, restoring us.

Our God, you see, is also our Savior—in Jesus Christ. How wonderful!

Be inspired by these truths as you read this week.

God is clothed with awesome majesty. . . He is great in power; justice and abundant righteousness he will not violate.

Job 37:22, 23

What makes a painting great? Or an opera? Or a pastry, for that matter? What makes an artist, a composer, a baker wonderful? How is that title earned?

By definition, a "wonderful" creation fills our hearts with wonder, with awe and appreciation:

- Consider the intricacies of light and color that dance on a canvas by Monet. Wonder-full!

- Or think about Verdi's opera *Aida*, often staged with enormous sets and sometimes even live horses. Wonder-full!

- Or contemplate that light-as-a-feather French pastry from your favorite bakery—cream-filled and coated with just enough dark chocolate. Wonder-full!

These things are wonderful. But the universe and its wonders are by far more awesome than anything any human being has ever produced. The raw power and intricate wisdom we see in the creation all around us arouse our wonder. But the physical aspects of creation are only the beginning.

Our Creator is also the source of all wisdom, of all beauty, of all truth, of all goodness! We know what justice is because God is just. We know what goodness is because our Creator is fully, entirely, steadfastly good.

Our hearts fill with wonder as we take this all in. Wonder and, perhaps, a dash of fear, as well. God is all-good, all-powerful, and all-just. In contrast, we are none of these things. We are often petty, selfish, mean.

Cracked sculptures, moldy pastries, broken oboe reeds—these are trashed. And rightly so. But destruction is not—and never was—our Creator's will for us. Instead, he intended to rescue, to ransom, to remake us. Writing about a different kind of reed, the prophet wrote:

He will not crush the weakest reed or put out a flickering candle.

Isaiah 42:3 NLT

We have no righteousness of our own. But the pure robe of our Savior's righteousness becomes ours by his grace, through faith. He clothes us in it. Jesus' very own righteousness belongs to all who simply believe his promise is true:

But now thus says the LORD, he who created you. . . . "Fear not, for I have redeemed you; I have called you by name, you are mine."

Isaiah 43:1

Our Creator is an awesome, wonder-full God. Think about that!

Prayer starter: Lord God, you are wonderful beyond my ability to imagine. Awesome. Majestic. Powerful. But above all, you are good. You made me and you forgive me . . .

Let all the earth fear the LORD; let all the inhabitants of the world stand in awe of him! For he spoke, and it came to be; he commanded, and it stood firm.

Psalm 33:8–9

A butterfly emerges from its chrysalis in the garden where the iris is about to bloom. We rush right by.

A snowflake—unique in all the world—lands on our jacket sleeve. We brush it off.

An orbiting satellite captures the indescribable colors of a nebula as it explodes hundreds of thousands of miles from Earth. The photos pop up on our news feed, covering our laptop screen. And we click right by.

Psychologists, life coaches, and pain management experts—all have made much about mindfulness in recent months. When we are mindful, we resist the temptation to rush, to brush off. When we are mindful, we pause. We stop to admire the wonders that lie before us.

As God's people, we have all the more reason to do this. The wonders around us are our heavenly Father's artistry! We admire the power, the creativity, the wisdom that mark his creation. And as we pause, we worship:

O LORD, how manifold are your works! In wisdom have you made them all; the earth is full of your creatures.

Psalm 104:24

Long before this current accent on mindfulness as a cure for the stress and strain of everyday life, the psalmist issued this invitation:

Let all the inhabitants of the world stand in awe of him!

Psalm 33:8

"Stop all this rushing!" the Bible urges us. "Stand still. Stand in awe of your Creator and of all that he has made, all that he has done, all that he is doing still."

Now, of course, some days are legitimately busy. Some activities are genuinely urgent. But at least some of the time, my own failures to stop, to stand still in awe, to rest, come from a heart that's too self-important and too doubtful of my heavenly Father's care for me. How about you?

In times like that, how wonderful it is to realize anew that our God is also our Savior. The wonders of nature invite our admiration. But the wonder of the cross leaves us breathless, speechless in amazement.

Mindful of the love Jesus showed for us on that cross, we worship. Attentive to the forgiveness and peace Jesus won for us there, we kneel in self-forgetful wonder.

Prayer starter: God, I need a break. I need to breathe deeply, if only for a moment, as I stand in awe of you, my Creator and my Savior . . .

You formed my inward parts; you knitted me together in my mother's womb. I praise you, for I am fearfully and wonderfully made. Wonderful are your works.

Psalm 139:13–14

The right tools make a task possible. Do you want to crochet? Then you need crochet hooks and specialized thread. Do you want to knit? Then you need knitting needles and yarn.

In both arts, the size of the hooks (or needles) must match the kind of thread (or yarn) you intend to use. And that, in turn, depends on what you intend to create.

So what kind of needles did your Creator use when he began to knit you together in your mother's womb? Of course, the Bible here is using a word picture, a metaphor. Right? Well . . . not so fast . . . keep this metaphor in mind as you find a diagram of DNA on your smartphone.

Do you see it? As I look at DNA diagrams, it seems this word picture may be a bit more literal than I had first imagined. DNA strands look quite a lot like yarn strands being woven together to make a scarf or baby blanket. Don't you think so, too?

And that's just the point! Our Creator works intentionally, like an artist. You are not the product of mindless forces set in motion by the random collision of sperm and egg. You were deliberately knitted together. Personally crafted. Individually made.

Your Creator gave you life itself. He ordered the details of your individual genes and guides their expression. He has done this from your very beginning, from before the moment you took your first breath.

Whether you were carried full term or were a preemie . . .

Whether you had brown or blond or red hair (or any hair at all) . . .

Whether you were wanted and dearly loved or abandoned by your human parents . . .

Your heavenly Father wanted you with all his heart. He cared for you—and still cares for you—with endless love, boundless compassion.

When sin and the circumstances of life in this sinful world spoiled his creations beyond recognition, he sent Jesus, his perfect Son—not to recall and destroy us but to make our complete restoration possible:

God did not send his Son into the world to condemn the world, but in order that the world might be saved through him. Whoever believes in him is not condemned.

John 3:17–18

Prayer starter: Thank you, Father, for the care you took as you made me. Teach me to care for . . .

9

For our sake he made him to be sin who knew no sin, so that in him we might become the righteousness of God.

2 Corinthians 5:21

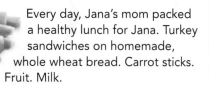

Every day, Jana's mom packed a healthy lunch for Jana. Turkey sandwiches on homemade, whole wheat bread. Carrot sticks. Fruit. Milk.

Every day, Jana exchanged her fruit for Michael's cupcakes. Every day, Jana exchanged her sandwich for Jorge's microwave mac and cheese. Every day, Jana exchanged her milk for Jill's pink lemonade.

Jana thought all these exchanges were great exchanges. Jana's mother would not have been so thrilled, had she ever learned what Jana was up to.

The words of 2 Corinthians 5:21 describe what some have called *the* Great Exchange. This passage describes what may be the wonder of all wonders. It can be hard for us to grasp the truth expressed here. The verse reads a lot like a riddle. Some background can help untangle it:

Jesus was no friend of sin. He was not even a distant acquaintance. He "knew no sin." He was holy, obedient, and right with God in every way.

You and I are on a first-name basis with sin. We know all about it. We are well acquainted with disobedience. Our friendship with rebellion goes way back.

In mercy, God the Father has subtracted all the sin—every single bit of it—from our account. He has replaced it with Jesus' very own righteousness.

Our sin did not just evaporate. God added our sin to Jesus' account. Jesus was punished for it on Calvary's cross.

With that as background, reread 2 Corinthians 5:21. It describes *the* Great Exchange. The greatest exchange ever! This is the Gospel message. This is the Good News that sets our hearts ablaze with joy and floods our lives with thanksgiving.

Not for his own benefit but for ours . . .

In deepest love for us . . .

God made Jesus—the One who never sinned . . .

Become sin itself.

Jesus became fully, totally, completely sinful . . .

So that now, in Jesus we are made fully holy, righteous, blameless before God!

This truth makes our re-creation possible!

Prayer starter: It's almost too good to be true, Lord! You took my sin and I received your righteousness. How can I thank you for remaking me? . . .

The Wonder of My Re-Creation

Beloved, we are God's children now, and what we will be has not yet appeared; but we know that when he appears we shall be like him, because we shall see him as he is.

1 John 3:2

Do you ever stop to think about what your first few minutes in heaven will be like? Have you ever asked yourself:

- What will be the first things I see and hear?

- What will it be like to be in the presence of Jesus, to really, actually see him?

- How will all this change me?

The Bible answers only a few of our many questions, but we know two things for sure:

- We will see Jesus "as he is" in all his grace, majesty, compassion, holiness, glory, and love.

- That experience will complete the process of our re-creation. We will "be like him," the apostle John promises. Fully. Forever.

John's promise builds on the words of King David, written a thousand years or so earlier:

As for me, I shall behold your face in righteousness; when I awake, I shall be satisfied with your likeness.

Psalm 17:15

David and John describe the same dynamic, the same sure-and-certain hope. This hope has belonged to all of God's people in every time and place. We will awaken to see our Savior's face. We will breathe a sigh of satisfaction, realizing the process of our re-creation is complete. We have become like our Savior.

Here on earth, we live as the forgiven, dearly loved children of God. The Holy Spirit has set up his home in our hearts. We have become God's construction site, as it were. He is remaking us, transforming us. The Bible describes our re-creation this way:

> *For we ourselves were once foolish, disobedient, led astray, slaves to various passions and pleasures, passing our days in malice and envy, hated by others and hating one another. But when the goodness and loving kindness of God our Savior appeared, he saved us.*
>
> Titus 3:3–5

These words are hard to read. It hurts my heart to think I was once like that—and sometimes still am. You, too?

The good news is that you and I are no longer who we once were! We have been remade! We are God's children now! Right now!

But we are not yet all that we are going to be. Our re-creation will be complete when we wake up in the presence of Christ. The best is yet to come. How wonderful!

Prayer starter: Thank you, Lord, that I am no longer who I once was. Continue to remake me so that I become more and more like Jesus . . .

With unequaled skill, care, and artistry, your Creator-God knitted you together in your mother's womb. It's wonderful!

He has also re-created you, bringing you to faith, making you his very own child, a member of his forever family. You are becoming more and more like your Brother, Jesus, day by day. How wonderful!

> Which of God's many creative works in nature do you consider most wonderful?

> Where do you see his re-creative work in your life right now, working repentance and faith in you?

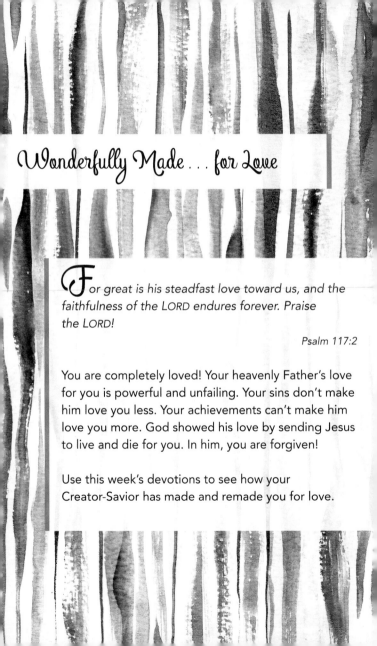

Wonderfully Made ... for Love

For great is his steadfast love toward us, and the faithfulness of the LORD endures forever. Praise the LORD!

Psalm 117:2

You are completely loved! Your heavenly Father's love for you is powerful and unfailing. Your sins don't make him love you less. Your achievements can't make him love you more. God showed his love by sending Jesus to live and die for you. In him, you are forgiven!

Use this week's devotions to see how your Creator-Savior has made and remade you for love.

See what kind of love the Father has given to us, that we should be called children of God; and so we are.

1 John 3:1

When I held my newborn daughter for the first time, I was surprised by how instantly and intensely I loved her. I'm not talking about the warm and fuzzy emotion of affection. Of course that was there, but this was something stronger. I immediately knew that I would do anything to ensure her well-being. My commitment isn't based on her personality, abilities, or how well she behaves. I love her because she is my child.

God describes his love for us as the love a father has for his child. His love is not just a feeling or an emotion. It's an active commitment. He stopped at nothing to provide for our well-being:

For God so loved the world, that he gave his only Son, that whoever believes in him should not perish but have eternal life.

John 3:16

In perfect love, God sent his only Son to save us from sin! It was something we could never have done on our own—only God's love could save us from the eternal consequences of our sin. And that love is never based on our actions. Nothing we do will make him love us more or less. God's love for us is based on the *perfect* goodness of Jesus.

God loved you even before he made you. He forgives you because of Christ's sacrifice. By faith in Jesus, you have been adopted into the family. You have been made a child of God!

Even before he made the world, God loved us and chose us in Christ to be holy and without fault in his eyes. . . . So we praise God for the glorious grace he has poured out on us who belong to his dear Son.

Ephesians 1:4, 6 NLT

The love I have for my children isn't perfect. I often slip into impatience and selfishness. I fail them in ways I don't even realize.

But God's love is different. No matter what kind of parents you have or don't have, God's love isn't limited by their example. Human parents may hurt or abandon their children, but God never does. God loves you more than any earthly parent could.

By the loving sacrifice of Jesus, you became God's forgiven and beloved daughter. You will spend eternity in perfect peace and joy with your heavenly Father. You were made for it!

Prayer starter: Heavenly Father, thank you for making me your child. Your love for me is perfect. Teach me to rely more and more on your love as I . . .

Therefore be imitators of God, as beloved children. And walk in love, as Christ loved us and gave himself up for us, a fragrant offering and sacrifice to God.

Ephesians 5:1–2

Have you ever seen children imitate their parents? Imagine a toddler dragging a purse along the floor as she shuffles across the house in high-heeled shoes. She wants to be "just like Mommy." Fast forward to adulthood and you can see a young woman using the same recipes and singing the same lullabies that she heard when she was young. Children may not even realize the things they learn from their parents. What began as imitation becomes a part of who they are.

As a forgiven child of God, love is a part of who you are. You are wholly and completely loved by your Creator. Your heavenly Father knows everything about you, even the stuff you'd like to hide. And he loves you anyway! His love is unconditional and transforming. Love that powerful can't help but overflow into your words and actions:

We love because he first loved us.

1 John 4:19

When you love others, you are merely reflecting what God has done for you. It's not your own light but his light of life that shines through you.

Jesus is the true source of light and love. He lived a life of love, serving the sick and poor. He died in love, unselfishly giving himself up by dying on the cross. Through his death and resurrection, all of your sins are forgiven. Every time you come to him in repentance, his love covers you and he forgives you again. He continues to serve you through his Word and strengthen you with his gifts. His love never ends!

As you strive to imitate Christ in the ways you show love to others, you will eventually come up short. Like a toddler wobbling on her mother's high heels, you will fall. That won't change God's love for you or his ability to work through you! God reaches down and pulls you up, while the Holy Spirit guides you on. Your heavenly Father works despite your weaknesses. By his perfect love, you are continually renewed—all because of Jesus. His love shines through you and it becomes a part of who you are.

Prayer starter: Heavenly Father, you showed me ultimate love by sending Jesus to redeem me. Day by day, remake me with your love, especially as I struggle to imitate you in . . .

Remade to Love in My Family

Since God chose you to be the holy people he loves, you must clothe yourselves with tenderhearted mercy, kindness, humility, gentleness, and patience. Make allowance for each other's faults, and forgive anyone who offends you. Remember, the Lord forgave you, so you must forgive others.

Colossians 3:12–13 NLT

Growing up with two brothers, I witnessed my fair share of squabbles. Screams of "That's my toy!" or "He pushed me!" were as common as bumps and bruises. As most parents would, mine required apologies after a fight. I often heard a monotone "I'm sorry" and a mumbled "I forgive you," followed by a mandatory handshake. The boys went through the motions, but it was clear their hearts weren't in it.

Unfortunately, those closest to us often get the worst of us. Family members use hurtful words and actions within their own homes that they would never use with others. Those who know you best have the greatest capacity to hurt you. Yet, the bonds created within a family can be stronger and longer lasting than any other. Co-workers and neighbors may come and go, but family connections can't be erased.

Navigating family relationships isn't easy. Apologies and forgiveness are a necessary (and often daily) part of healthy family life. But what if there isn't an apology? What if forgiveness isn't deserved? How can you forgive someone who just doesn't deserve it? There are conflicts that just can't be resolved and differences that can't be settled. Sometimes the only way to build a healthy relationship is to forgive and love anyway.

Forgiveness is possible only through the power of God. His love enables you to give what isn't deserved or even asked for. You can forgive others only because the Lord has forgiven you. Before you even asked for it, Jesus earned your complete forgiveness. God sent Jesus to pay the price for your sins.

God shows his love for us in that while we were still sinners, Christ died for us.

Romans 5:8

You don't deserve God's forgiveness, but in Jesus, you have it. You have it filled to the brim and overflowing with more than enough to share!

You and I can never love and forgive to the extent that God loves and forgives us. Like fighting children, we often go through the motions of giving and receiving apologies. Thankfully, our weaknesses don't erase God's strength! He works through our attempts to love our family and forgives us when we fail. In Jesus, you have total forgiveness—filled to the brim and overflowing!

Prayer starter: Jesus, you selflessly earned my forgiveness on the cross. Help me share your love and forgiveness with my family, especially in my relationship with . . .

21

Remade to Love in My Community

Whatever you do, work heartily, as for the Lord.

Colossians 3:23

I once had a neighbor whose dog loved my backyard. He loved it so much that he made regular visits. No matter how many times I politely asked my neighbor to keep his dog in his own yard, I would continually find evidence of the dog's presence on my property. The ongoing frustration put a strain on my relationship with my neighbor. Friendly small talk was replaced with a forced smile and nod. I began to feel that my neighbor didn't deserve my time or effort anymore.

You may not always love your neighbors, but God does. You may consider some people in your community to be unworthy of your time and effort, but God doesn't. God loves each person in your community no matter his or her faults, weaknesses, or sins. The question isn't "Who *deserves* my acts of service?" but rather "Who *needs* my acts of service?"

Looking for the needs in your community and working to meet those needs is a powerful witness to God's love. As you forgive your neighbor, you show that God's love is for everyone, everywhere. No limits, no boundaries, no fences.

Your community needs you because it needs to see the truth of God's love in your actions. Your witness begins as you treat your neighbors with love and respect despite your differences. Even the smallest acts of service point others to Christ; smiling, listening, shoveling snow, and cutting grass all reflect God's love.

God showed his perfect love for you without considering your worthiness. He sent Jesus to die on the cross even though you didn't deserve it. Through faith in him you are given eternal life, not because of anything you did but because of what he did for you!

God's love remakes you from the inside out.

We are his workmanship, created in Christ Jesus.

Ephesians 2:10

In Christ Jesus, you can serve your community without considering its worthiness. In Christ Jesus, you can love your inconsiderate neighbor. In Christ Jesus, you can display God's love to the hurting world.

When you serve others, you serve God. When you love others, you live out your love for God. It all comes from him, because of him, for him!

Prayer starter: Lord, thank you for loving me and sending Jesus to pay the price for my sins. Please work through me when I show that love to my community as I . . .

Remade to Love in My Church Family

Addressing one another in psalms and hymns and spiritual songs, singing and making melody to the Lord with your heart, giving thanks always and for everything to God the Father in the name of our Lord Jesus Christ, submitting to one another out of reverence for Christ.

Ephesians 5:19–21

"Come over next week and I'll show you how to make homemade applesauce."

The invitation caught me off guard. I was making small talk with an older woman at church, sharing about my trip to the orchard that weekend and the overflowing drawer of apples in my refrigerator. I didn't expect her to take much interest in it; we were just chatting. I was taken aback by her offer. Being friendly at church is one thing, but an invitation to her home is another.

"Feel free to bring the baby and spend the afternoon," she added. I accepted.

We became friends, and over time, she became a mentor in my life. She treated me more like a family member than the person in the pew next to her. I continue to look to her as a role model of what it means to be a Christian woman in a stage of life I've yet to enter. The time and energy she's invested in our friendship has helped me grow in my faith and find new ways to serve the Lord.

It's easy to breeze in and out of church on Sunday mornings without giving much thought to those around you: a little small talk, some handshakes or hugs, and home before lunch. But the community of believers is much more than a group of random people who come together for an hour on Sunday. God's Church is a family!

Consider taking the time to get to know someone in your congregation. Starting a conversation might be stepping out of your comfort zone, but with God's help, it is worth it. The young woman sitting alone each week, the elderly couple up front, the high school boy sitting with his grandma, the single mom juggling three kids—they are all members of your family.

Through the death of Jesus, you have been forgiven and adopted as children of God. As brothers and sisters in Christ, you have the opportunity to love and support each other. Sometimes that means praying for each other, talking throughout the week, or meeting for Bible study. And sometimes, it even means making applesauce together.

Prayer starter: How wonderful, Lord, that you support and encourage me through my church family! This week, I want to reach out in love to . . .

You were made for love, made to receive God's limitless, life-changing love for you in Jesus Christ. It's wonderful!

"But can God's love possibly be for *me*?" we ask. Yes, the Bible says. None of us deserves God's love, but it is ours even so:

God shows his love for us in that while we were still sinners, Christ died for us.

Romans 5:8

How wonderful!

In what ways does knowing God's no-matter-what love change how you relate to him?

How does God's love for you change your love for others?

Wonderfully Made... for Joy

Have you ever played the "Spot the Difference" puzzles in a newspaper? There are two pictures that at first glance appear identical, but when you look closer, there are differences between the two.

At first glance, happiness and joy appear to be the same thing. But if you look closer, they're different. True joy from God is deep, abiding, and lasting—no matter the circumstances.

This week, see how faith in Jesus brings us joy, so much joy that we can't help but share it!

Made for Joy

But the righteous shall be glad; they shall exult before God; they shall be jubilant with joy!

Psalm 68:3

"Betcha can't eat just one." The Frito-Lay company introduced this slogan for its Lay's potato chips in the 1960s. It is a memorable advertising campaign because it presents a challenge, maybe even a dare. Frito-Lay is saying that its chips are so good, it is impossible to eat just one. Barbecue flavor? Betcha can't eat just one. Sour cream and onion? Betcha can't eat just one. New England lobster roll? Pimento cheese? Betcha can't eat just one.

God our heavenly Father could issue us, his children, a similar challenge: Betcha can't not have joy. Okay, it doesn't really roll off your tongue, but it's true. As a child of God, we were made for joy. King David tells us so in Psalm 68:3:

The righteous shall be glad. . . . They shall be jubilant with joy!

But this joy, this jubilation, is reserved for one type of people: the righteous. Do you count yourself among the righteous? Do you get lost in your own selfish ways, chasing after worldly desires and fleeting happiness? Ever find yourself putting all your trust in things you *think* will bring you joy: professional success, material possessions, popularity, children, or hobbies?

Our sins have a way of deceiving us and snatching happiness away, just when it seems within reach. But the righteousness we need, and the unsurpassable joy that accompanies it, comes through a relationship with God, our Creator. And we can have that relationship only through Jesus. In our sin, we were separated from God, but Jesus' work on the cross has brought us back, redeemed us, and made us righteous by faith in his name!

But now God has shown us a way to be made right with him. . . . We are made right with God by placing our faith in Jesus Christ. And this is true for everyone who believes, no matter who we are. For everyone has sinned; we all fall short of God's glorious standard. Yet God, in his grace, freely makes us right in his sight. He did this through Christ Jesus when he freed us from the penalty for our sins.

Romans 3:21–24 NLT

David says the righteous shall be glad, and thank God, we have been made righteous in Jesus! How can we not be jubilant with joy? In Jesus we are wonderfully made for joy!

Prayer starter: Holy Creator, thank you for making me right with you in Jesus. Remind me that I am made for joy even when I feel . . .

Made to Rejoice

Rejoice in the Lord always; again I will say, rejoice.

Philippians 4:4

When we watch or read the news, it's hard to find good things happening. War rages and civilians suffer from starvation and disease. Wildfires destroy homes and businesses. Floods and hurricanes sweep away livelihoods and treasured memories. Governments imprison dissenters and violently persecute missionaries.

Now look closer. Are you being bullied at work? Are you or a family member struggling to keep a marriage together? Are you watching a child, spouse, or co-worker caught in the claws of addiction?

It's easy to rejoice and praise God when things are going well; it's much harder to rejoice in times of suffering.

The apostle Paul knew about suffering. He was imprisoned not once but twice, before ultimately being executed. Today's Bible verse comes from Paul's letter to the church at Philippi. When he wrote it, he was likely under house arrest, under constant surveillance and unable to move about freely. He was a prisoner, yet he was encouraging his readers to rejoice!

Your Savior, Jesus, also knew what it was to suffer. He suffered beatings and death on a cross, but he also grieved the death of his friend Lazarus. He watched with anger as money changers desecrated the temple. He saw the pain of the blind, the lame, and the demon possessed. He ate with society's outcasts—prostitutes and tax collectors. Jesus walked in our broken world and knew our human pain, experiencing much of it himself.

But just as Paul rejoiced in suffering, we, too, as Jesus' followers, are made to rejoice in all circumstances. We can rejoice in the face of hardship because we are not alone— our Savior walks with us. Because Jesus has promised us everlasting life, we can rejoice in our suffering—we know it is only temporary.

Most of all, we know we are made to rejoice because rejoicing brings glory to God! When we rejoice in good times and in struggles, we acknowledge God's glory in our lives and in our world. He is in control and promises to work everything for the good of his creation (Romans 8:28). We are made to rejoice in God our Savior, always.

Prayer starter: Dear Lord, help me rejoice in all circumstances, especially as I deal with . . .

Remade to Bring Joy in Heaven

Just so, I tell you, there will be more joy in heaven over one sinner who repents than over ninety-nine righteous persons who need no repentance.

Luke 15:7

Think of a concert you've attended. Whether it was at a county fair, in a hockey stadium, or in a concert venue, all concerts have certain elements in common: there is an audience and an artist. The audience is excited because of what it's about to see. Maybe some of the audience members have bought a band t-shirt. Maybe some people have driven hundreds of miles to attend. Excitement pulses and buzzes through the venue until finally the band takes the stage. The audience jumps to its feet and applause fills the air. During the show, all the way to the end, the cheering and clapping continue.

Now imagine instead of a concert hall, it's heaven, and instead of a band, all the holy angels are cheering for and rejoicing over a sinner who has repented. Boisterous, manic, vigorous clapping; loud whistles; and energized hoots fill the air because one person turned away from sin.

Luke 15 starts with the parable of the lost sheep. Jesus tells the story of a man who has 100 sheep. One goes missing, and without skipping a beat, the shepherd leaves the 99 sheep to go find the one who wandered off. That one sheep was so precious to the shepherd that he refused to abandon it to the elements, but instead, he went after it. Then, when he found it, he invited his friends and neighbors to come and rejoice with him.

You are a cherished daughter of God, so special to him that he would never leave you in your sinfulness. Instead, he goes looking for you when you wander away. He reaches out to you in the person of his only Son, the Good Shepherd, Jesus. He searches high and low until he finds you and once he does, does he shame you or give you the silent treatment? No! Jesus rejoices, together with all the throng of heaven as you confess your sin, turn from it, and return to God. Jesus forgives us and welcomes us back into the flock with open arms!

The forgiveness we have in Jesus is something we can share with others. We can forgive those who have let us down, just as Jesus forgives us when we go astray. Praise God for the joy that is ours—and heaven's—when one sinner repents!

Prayer starter: Forgiving Jesus, remind me that you are the Good Shepherd who comes to find me when I wander off. Help me show your forgiveness to . . .

Remade to Bring Joy on Earth

For what thanksgiving can we return to God for you, for all the joy that we feel for your sake before our God.

1 Thessalonians 3:9

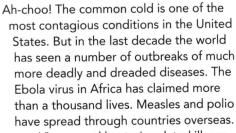

Ah-choo! The common cold is one of the most contagious conditions in the United States. But in the last decade the world has seen a number of outbreaks of much more deadly and dreaded diseases. The Ebola virus in Africa has claimed more than a thousand lives. Measles and polio have spread through countries overseas. Viruses and bacteria-related illness can be highly contagious, passing from one unsuspecting person to another until it seems like everyone is sick.

Why does it seem like only harmful things are contagious? Wouldn't it be wonderful, for example, if joy were contagious? Maybe you've experienced something close to that. Have you ever found yourself in a conversation in which someone starts laughing and then, seemingly out of nowhere, everyone is laughing? It's the kind of laughter you can't stop. You're not even totally sure why you're laughing, but your cheeks hurt, your belly aches.

In today's Bible verse, Paul tells the church at Thessalonica that he thanks God for them and that he feels great joy when he thinks about how they are growing as faithful Christians. Throughout 1 Thessalonians, Paul uses expressions of paternal love. In the same way a father says, "I'm so proud of you," Paul expresses his pleasure at hearing the church is holding up in the face of persecution and is not falling away into false beliefs. The church is bringing Paul joy even though he is writing from far away.

As the loved and forgiven children of God, we are called to share the joy we have because of our relationship with Jesus. We're called to spread that joy as far and wide as a preschooler spreads pink eye. It's not a hard job! Jesus loves you so much that he willingly left his throne in heaven to endure the trials of this sinful world. By faith in Jesus, in his sacrificial death and in his triumphant resurrection, we will live forever. How can you not share that joy!

We can spread our joy in Jesus by walking away from negative or gossip-filled conversations at work. We can spread the joy by offering a kind word to a friend who is struggling. We can spread the joy by simply sitting with a loved one who is in the hospital. Our joy is made to be contagious because the joy we have is eternal and it comes from Jesus. It's joy worth spreading!

Prayer starter: Dear Jesus, show me how to spread the contagious joy of your love this week as I . . .

And the ransomed of the LORD shall return and come to Zion with singing; everlasting joy shall be upon their heads; they shall obtain gladness and joy, and sorrow and sighing shall flee away.

Isaiah 35:10

Where do you see yourself in five years? Maybe you'll be retired. Maybe you'll get that promotion you want. Maybe you'll be able to quit your job to stay home and take care of your family. How about in 15 years? Will you be packing up and dropping your child off at college? Maybe you'll be attending a grandchild's dance recital. Maybe you'll be boarding a plane for that tropical vacation you've been planning.

Here's perhaps a more interesting question: Where do you see yourself in 500 years?

We plan for the future. We have things we want to accomplish. We have places we want to go. We want to make a difference. Along the way we will experience joy. You may experience the joy of adopting a new puppy. You may experience the joy of watching a child in your Sunday school class come to faith in Jesus. You may experience the joy of finally paying off your mortgage or your student loans. But what about eternity? How often do you think about forever?

You see, we are not temporary creatures; we are God's eternal creations. Our eternal life does not start when we die, or it wouldn't be eternal. The dictionary defines *eternal* as "continuing without interruption; perpetual." Our eternal life began the day we became a child of God by faith and continues without interruption, even the interruption of death.

How often, though, do we live as if the part of our eternal life we are living right now is all there is? We worry about things we cannot control. We blow problems out of proportion, failing to trust God is powerful enough and wise enough to handle them. We allow ourselves to be mired in sadness, forgetting God's promise to reunite us with our faith family in heaven. We stockpile possessions, relying on them for security, rather than trusting God for it. We allow anger to consume us, instead of looking to our heavenly Father to mete out justice in his time.

But as redeemed and eternal children of God, we can lay all of that down and pick up the eternal joy we have in Jesus. Isaiah prophesied that the Lord's people would come into heaven with singing and that everlasting, unending, uninterrupted joy would be theirs. That same eternal joy is yours. As a child of God you were made for joy—joy on earth and joy in heaven forever.

Prayer starter: Thank you, O Lord, for creating me for joy and for giving me everlasting joy in my Savior, Jesus. Help me to remember that when it's hard, especially when . . .

Wonderful Joy

You were not made for gloom and doom. No, God created you for joy! It's wonderful!

"Can this possibly be—for *me*?" we ask. Yes, the Bible says, describing joy's source:

Though you do not now see him, you believe in him and rejoice with joy that is inexpressible and filled with glory.

1 Peter 1:8

Our joy is in Jesus. Always and forever! How wonderful!

What words do you use to describe the joy Jesus brings you?

In what way is that joy too big for words?

Wonderfully Made . . . for Service

What makes Christian service special? Everything!

From the "who" to the "what" to the "why," serving in God's name is unique, totally contrary to the world's expectations.

We serve our friends . . . and our enemies. We move as the Holy Spirit guides us, even though we're unsure of our destination. We do it all, following the ultimate Servant, who shows us how.

Your service—all to God's glory—is the focus this week.

Praise the LORD! Praise the name of the LORD, give praise, O servants of the LORD.

Psalm 135:1

A woman on a diet facing a dessert buffet: "Oh, wow, I'm going to eat that triple-chocolate cake. I just can't help it!"

A young child ripping through his birthday presents so quickly that his parents can't keep up: "I'm so excited! I just can't help it!"

A teenager thinking about stealing high-priced sneakers: "I don't have enough money, but I *have* to have those shoes. I just can't help it!"

We sometimes use this phrase when we know we shouldn't do something but feel our entire being pushing us toward that one thing. Chocolate cake, presents, high-priced shoes—it doesn't matter. The pull is undeniable and, seemingly, irresistible!

Our original, unblemished calling is to work in service to God, to serve God by serving those around us. That's what we are created to do! Genesis 2:15 tells us that God put Adam and Eve into the Garden of Eden to "work it and keep it."

But, while Eve was supposed to be busy maintaining Paradise, along came temptation. Eve knew she shouldn't eat from the tree of the knowledge of good and evil—God had explicitly told her not to do it. Even so, the pull was undeniable, seemingly irresistible. She had to eat that fruit—she just couldn't help it!

When sin entered the world, it wiped out our unblemished will to serve God. We may serve our neighbor—but only when it's convenient for us. We may volunteer for leadership positions at church—but only to pad our resumes. On our own, our heart for service looks nothing like what God had in mind when he created us.

Selfish service came to a screeching halt when our Savior entered the world. From his humble birth to his death on the cross, Jesus lived as servant of all. Everything he did was to glorify his Father in heaven. Everything he did was to show his love for God's people. He just couldn't help it.

Because of Jesus' death and resurrection, we have received a new heart for service. We were made for service, and because of Jesus, we can fulfill that calling from God—and do it joyfully!

Serving others is no longer a "have to" but a "get to." We get to glorify God! We get to help and serve those around us! We get to spread the love of Jesus through our selfless acts of service! Praise the Lord—we just can't help it!

Prayer starter: Heavenly Father, forgive me for those times when I serve selfishly. Put a "get to" attitude in my heart so that I may praise you through . . .

Made to Serve

Let us not grow weary of doing good, for in due season we will reap, if we do not give up. So then, as we have opportunity, let us do good to everyone, and especially to those who are of the household of faith.

Galatians 6:9–10

You've probably seen the comical fitness advertisements from the 1920s. A high-heeled lady stood on a platform with a vibrating belt around her backside. The jiggling belt promised to shake the lady's body into shape. All she had to do was stand there!

You may be surprised to know that these vibrating fitness machines have come a long way in the past century. Yes, they do still exist. But are they any more effective than the odd-looking belt from way back when? Medical experts say, "No."

The reason is pretty logical: if you want the benefits of exercise, you have to move your body.

A similar connection exists between our faith and good works: our faith moves us to serve. Our Christian walk is dull and lifeless if we sit idle. God created our hearts and bodies to move, to step out in service!

The apostle Paul tells us to "consider [ourselves] dead to sin and alive to God in Christ Jesus" (Romans 6:11). Dead versus alive. Idle versus active. Sitting versus serving. The choice is yours every day.

God didn't send his only Son to live a perfect life in your place and die your death upon the cross so that you could keep your faith pristinely tied up in a neat package, never using it or bringing it out for others to see. No, your heavenly Father made you to use your faith in service each and every day!

[Jesus] gave his life to free us from every kind of sin, to cleanse us, and to make us his very own people, totally committed to doing good deeds.

Titus 2:14 NLT

God made you, in Christ, to be "totally committed" to serving others. If that sounds intimidating to you, you're not alone. After a long day of work, are you totally committed to caring for your teething infant? After serving on your church's Sunday school board for three years, are you totally committed to another three years?

We all grow weary in service. Even Jesus grew tired as he served people during his earthly ministry. He had exhausting days. He pulled away. He needed time alone. He knows your struggles! When you are weary, when you feel as if you have nothing more to give, go to your Savior and Friend. He promises to refresh your heart and strengthen you for continued service in his name.

Prayer starter: Lord Jesus, as you have served me, help me to move forward in faith and service. Holy Spirit, set my heart ablaze as I serve . . .

So, whether you eat or drink, or whatever you do, do all to the glory of God.

1 Corinthians 10:31

Renowned business consultant and motivational speaker Simon Sinek has made millions of dollars by teaching one simple concept: the most important thing isn't *what* we do but *why* we do it.

Even though 40 million YouTube viewers consider Sinek's thinking to be revolutionary, we see in today's Bible verse that Paul had the secret to fulfillment figured out almost 2,000 years ago: "Do all to the glory of God."

This is our purpose in serving, in life! But all too often, we get lost in the sea of legalism. We try to abide by a list of Christian do's and don'ts. In self-righteousness we value God's Law above God himself, our loving Father and Creator.

Our sole purpose, why we do what we do, becomes following the Bible. We serve because the Law tells us to serve. We serve to become the perfect Christian, perhaps even to put ourselves on a pedestal above other believers. But serving with purposes like these—to achieve self-styled perfection and self-righteousness—is empty service. There's no love. There's no heart. There's really no purpose at all.

If all we had was the Law, this would be the end of the story. This would be our "why."

But your service has a much deeper meaning—to give glory to God! Because we've been remade in Jesus, our service takes on a whole new purpose. We stop looking for fulfillment in the Law and turn to the One who has already fulfilled the Law—completely. We depend on Jesus for our purpose in service. Because of our Savior, we have a grace-filled purpose!

In his life and death in our place, Jesus satisfied the requirements of the Law for us, something we would never be able to do. Now, God sees you and all of your service as perfect. You can scrub floors—to the glory of God! You can babysit your grandchildren—to the glory of God! You can work as a rocket scientist—to the glory of God!

Your tendency to lose sight of your purpose and rely on your own self-righteousness instead of on the righteousness Jesus won for you on the cross is probably frustrating. You might look back with embarrassment on the times you grumbled and dragged your feet in service. In times like that, you can turn to your loving Servant and Friend, Jesus, for forgiveness. He promises to cleanse your heart and restore your spirit for service. And you can look forward to the day you will serve God in endless bliss in heaven. Sin will be no more and your service will be perfect (Revelation 22:3).

Prayer starter: Heavenly Father, guide my thoughts so that my "why" will always be focused on you. Remake my heart so that I will serve others with a spirit of . . .

May the Lord make you increase and abound in love for one another and for all, as we do for you, so that he may establish your hearts blameless in holiness before our God and Father, at the coming of our Lord Jesus with all his saints.

1 Thessalonians 3:12–13

The Argus II is a bionic eye.

No, this isn't from some science-fiction movie—it's real. The unit looks like a fairly standard pair of sunglasses, just with a few extra attachments. But what it does is remarkable. The Argus II mimics normal eye function by providing a specialized electrical stimulation of the retina. Although the vision created by this bionic eye isn't full and robust, it gives formerly blind individuals a stunning view of the world around them.

Even though most of us have a pair of fully functioning retinas, we are quite blind at times. And not even the most technologically advanced sunglasses will help us.

Consider a typical day. You get up, go about your business, come home, and go to bed. But did you see the dishwasher? You could've unloaded it so your husband didn't have to do it when he got home from a 12-hour shift. Did you see your elderly neighbor's trash can at the curb? You could've taken it back to his garage. Did you see the co-worker that's been working 50 hours a week, the friend who just had a baby, or the mail carrier juggling three packages?

You missed all of these opportunities to serve because of a blindness—sin-induced blindness. In selfishness, even we as Christians often put our needs above the needs of those closest to us. We value busyness and the sense of self-importance it creates as we rush right past those who need us most. We doubt our God-given gifts and foolishly think that God doesn't care if we serve or not.

Let God open your eyes to service! He wants to "make you increase and abound in love for one another and for all" (1 Thessalonians 3:12). You can't see without him, but as you walk in faith, the Holy Spirit will guide your heart to recognize these opportunities for heartfelt service. And he will multiply your joy in serving again and again!

We see and we learn from our Savior, Jesus:

> *Let each of you look not only to his own interests, but also to the interests of others. Have this mind among yourselves, which is yours in Christ Jesus, who, though he was in the form of God, did not count equality with God a thing to be grasped, but emptied himself, by taking the form of a servant, being born in the likeness of men.*
>
> *Philippians 2:4–7*

Ask Jesus to help you leave behind your self-focus. Ask him to empty your selfish heart. Then, filled by the love he showed at Calvary's cross, begin looking to the needs of others. Pour your heart into serving those around you—at your workplace, in your community, in your church, in your home. You will see the world differently. And when you see, then you can serve.

Prayer starter: Jesus, give me eyes to see those around me who need my love and service the most. Forgive my selfishness and lead me to . . .

Remade to Serve Those Far Away

They gave themselves first to the Lord and then by the will of God to us.

2 Corinthians 8:5

In today's Bible verse, Paul is writing to the church in Corinth, located in the southern part of Greece. This verse describes Christians who lived in the northern part of Greece, an area called Macedonia. A great distance divided the believers in Corinth from those in Macedonia, but Paul was relying on both churches to provide money to combat the poverty being experienced by a third group of believers—the church in Jerusalem.

Those in Macedonia knew a thing or two about being poor. They were the poorest of the poor. On top of that, they were suffering persecution. They were certainly not people you'd expect to provide enthusiastic donations that would benefit people more than a thousand miles away.

But enthusiasm for giving was exactly what they had!

The people in Macedonia were devoted to doing God's will—no matter what. They saw giving as a privilege—no matter how difficult it was or how uncomfortable it made them. They weren't going to allow anything to get in the way of their service to their Lord and Savior.

In service to God, the Macedonians served people far away, believers from a totally different country. You and I don't have to travel to another country to find people that are "far away." Unbelievers at work, people in prisons or halfway houses, poor people, rich people, people who make us uncomfortable, people we disagree with—these are the people that for us are "far away." And they need our service just as much as the people who are close to us.

Jesus was an expert at serving people far away. He ate with sinners who made other people uncomfortable. He blessed the children, individuals whom other adults mostly ignored. And in an ultimate act of service, he washed the feet of his betrayer.

In John 13, we read about when Jesus washed his disciples' feet just hours before he would be sentenced to death. We read with anticipation; what will Jesus do when he gets to Judas? He treated his betrayer in the same way he treated the other disciples; Jesus washed Judas' feet.

How angry would you be if God called you to serve in ways similar to the ways Jesus served that night? Would you serve the person who was about to send you to your death? For us, it's unfathomable. For Jesus, it's proof.

It's proof of Jesus' selfless, unbounded love for us. It's proof that God is willing to go as far as it takes to bring his rebellious creations into his family. Jesus is at work when things get uncomfortable. His glory and his love aren't meant to be shared only in our homes and churches. We are meant to serve *all types of people* with his love.

Commit your service to the Lord, wherever it—and he—may take you.

Prayer starter: Dear God, sometimes I'm afraid to serve. I don't know what to say or how to act. Sometimes I just don't want to do it. Lord, work in my heart . . .

God created you to make a difference. He intends that you find joy in honoring him—your Creator, your Savior—in your service for others. It's wonderful!

You may say, "I have no special gifts, no truly useful abilities." But whenever your Lord asks you to serve, he equips you for that service. How wonderful!

In what ways are you using your God-given abilities to help his people?

List times you have found genuine joy in serving others. What can you learn from your list?

Wonderfully Made . . . for Witness

The word *witness* usually carries two distinct meanings. It functions as either a noun or a verb in the English language. As a noun, *witness* refers to a person who experienced a particular event. As a verb, *witness* refers to the action of testifying or telling what a person knows.

So what does it mean then that we've been wonderfully made to witness? Let's find out this week!

Made for Witness

Paul, a servant of Christ Jesus, called to be an apostle, set apart for the gospel of God.

Romans 1:1

To a child, it looked like any other cheap plastic trinket—a simple cross with "Jesus Saves" printed on it. Immense disappointment draped itself over my small shoulders, making them droop. A quick search of the gift wrapping netted nothing else. Turning my attention back to the gift, I saw that the thin, plastic cross measured only about four inches in height and less than two inches in width. The cross, a Christmas gift, seemed like much too ordinary a gift coming from someone I regarded as the best teacher ever. And then she explained, "Set the cross in the sunlight, and when it's dark, the cross may surprise you!"

I dutifully placed my plastic cross in a bedroom window, and, being only a child, I promptly forgot all about it. The sun shone on the unwanted gift throughout the day. When the lights went out at bedtime, I noticed a small, soft light coming from my window. It was the plastic cross. It glowed in the dark!

Today's Bible verse reminds me of the glow-in-the-dark cross. By setting that cross aside in the sun, its true value and purpose was revealed. God, our heavenly Father, has set us apart, too! Read Romans 1:1 again, but this time, replace Paul's name with your own.

Surprised? It's true! Your identity is firmly established because our almighty God has set you apart! The great

Creator of all that exists has made you to be a servant of Christ Jesus. The word *servant* is sometimes translated as "slave," but in this case it doesn't carry the common connotations of brutality or drudgery. Instead, the word *servant* expresses the notion of specialness. It's a most high honor to be a servant of Christ! What a distinct (and humbling) privilege—that God has set you apart to serve the Savior of the world!

As Christ's servant, you are called to be an advocate, a promoter, a Gospel proclaimer. Wait! What? Yes, you read that right! God has set you apart to declare the truth about the One you serve—Jesus! God has set you apart so that you can witness! Your message? Jesus saves!

Prayer starter: Dear God, you've set me apart for a purpose. Give me grace to live as one set apart to witness, especially when . . .

You will receive power when the Holy Spirit has come upon you, and you will be my witnesses in Jerusalem and in all Judea and Samaria, and to the end of the earth.

Acts 1:8

Have you ever tossed a stone into calm lake waters? Or watched what happens when a drop of rain falls into a puddle? Even the smallest break in the water's surface will cause ripples to form. Beginning at the point of disturbance, a circular wave will immediately surround the point of impact. Each ripple continues outward from the center, ever enlarging itself as it moves faster and faster. Many more circular ripple waves follow the first one, making the stone's impact felt far from where it originally hit the water. A single small stone or water droplet can affect a very large area on the water's surface.

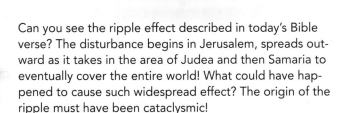

Can you see the ripple effect described in today's Bible verse? The disturbance begins in Jerusalem, spreads outward as it takes in the area of Judea and then Samaria to eventually cover the entire world! What could have happened to cause such widespread effect? The origin of the ripple must have been cataclysmic!

Actually, it began with a haphazard parade. Jesus entered Jerusalem, knowing what lay ahead, but his friends and followers never could have guessed that the coming days would make a tsunami-size impact throughout the entire world. Passersby mistakenly thought everything ended at Golgotha as Jesus cried, "It is finished!" (John 19:30). But three days later, the earth's foundations shook as life overcame death—forever!

News of Jesus' life, death, and resurrection surged throughout Jerusalem. Disciples and apostles carried the Gospel message out from Jerusalem to Judea and Samaria and beyond. And the ripple of forgiveness and eternal life still flows! It laps at your feet now and it comes to you with a declaration by Jesus himself: "You will be my witnesses."

With these five words Jesus gives your life purpose and direction. You were made for this! What's more, Jesus gives you a wonderful promise: "You will receive power when the Holy Spirit has come upon you."

The Holy Spirit enables and invigorates your witness. He gives you courage, wisdom, and strength. The Spirit brings you to opportunities and makes your words of witness effective. Riding along on the ripple waves, you are propelled by the Holy Spirit, and by grace, you get to participate in the work God created for you to do.

Prayer starter: Dear Jesus, pour out your Holy Spirit on me. Help me see myself as your witness when . . .

Remade to Witness God at Work

By grace you have been saved through faith. And this is not your own doing; it is the gift of God, not a result of works, so that no one may boast.

Ephesians 2:8–9

The witness raised her right hand and swore to tell the truth, the whole truth, and nothing but the truth. She promised to tell what she had seen with her own eyes. She agreed to relay just the facts, as she knew them. The witness's testimony would not include any personal opinions or assumptions. She swore not to exaggerate or downplay what she'd witnessed. Her words would convey truth, so help her God.

The testimony of an eyewitness is very powerful. It carries such weight because the jury hears about the accident or crime from someone who was at the scene. A witness is one who has personally observed an incident taking place. Then, she relays the information as clearly and thoroughly as possible.

Ephesians 2:8–9 reminds us that we are simply bystanders or witnesses when it comes to our own salvation. All by himself, God in grace sent Jesus to die for us. By faith, we now belong to the family of God. We've done nothing to secure our salvation. We can be certain of our complete forgiveness and eternal life because God himself has accomplished it!

In sending his Son, Jesus, God demonstrates his determination and grace—love that none of us deserves but which he freely offers! Even our faith is a gift, the Bible tells us.

The very act of believing and trusting in Jesus for forgiveness and salvation are gifts. We are witnesses to these gifts, but have done nothing to deserve any of it.

Here's where our relationship with our gracious God differs from every other relationship we'll ever experience. Nothing we do will cause God to love us more than he already does. Nothing! In fact, our good deeds are regarded as nothing more than filthy rags in the presence of a holy God (Isaiah 64:6).

And here's the greatest news of all: nothing we do will cause God to love us any less than the amazing way he loves us now! Why? Because all of our sins have been covered through the blood of Jesus, our Savior. Every. Sin. Covered. Completely.

Prayer starter: It's hard to even imagine how much you love me, Lord. Remind me of your grace today, and help me extend that grace as I . . .

But you are a chosen race, a royal priesthood, a holy nation, a people for his own possession, that you may proclaim the excellencies of him who called you out of darkness into his marvelous light.

1 Peter 2:9

Describe yourself in 25 words or less. Will you mention your name and tell about your family? Or, maybe name your occupation or identify where you grew up. It's probably safe to say that you wouldn't include the words of 1 Peter 2:9! And yet, this *is* who you are!

Through the atoning work of Jesus, believers in the Savior are welcomed into the family of God. Our ethnicity is irrelevant. We are now, through Jesus, God's "chosen race."

Believers in Christ share his regal bloodline. As part of the "royal priesthood" we are free to approach God, our heavenly Father, without an intercessory. Picture the Spirit searching for you as you fearfully sit in the absolute darkness of your sin. Now see Jesus reaching down into the dark pit of eternal death and extending his nail-scarred hand to pluck you out. The light is so marvelous that at first you can't bear it! Suddenly you hear your heavenly Father declaring, "You're mine now. Forever."

Darkness to light. We no longer cower in fear. We stand tall because we're forgiven. Deliverance brings overwhelming gratitude and something more. It's the urge to tell about it—coming from darkness into God's marvelous light!

Believers in Jesus are proclaimers—witnesses to the excellency of God. Look and see what God's Word has to say about witnessing through our words:

Pray also for us, that God may open to us a door for the word, to declare the mystery of Christ.

Colossians 4:3

Pray for a witnessing opportunity. Often, a chance to talk about faith springs from what's going on in your life, in the life of a friend, or in the world. Watch for the Spirit to provide an opportunity for a natural witness—an honest, transparent, and humble witness.

Tell *your* faith story. It's inevitably connected to the story of Jesus, the Savior.

I am not ashamed of this Good News about Christ. It is the power of God at work, saving everyone who believes.

Romans 1:16 NLT

Pray that the Holy Spirit will work through your witnessing words to create faith in your listener's heart.

Remember who you are in Christ. You are chosen, royal, and holy. And most important of all, you are his!

Prayer starter: Holy Spirit, give me the opportunity, the courage, and just the right words to speak about Jesus today. Some people you bring to mind right now include . . .

For we are God's masterpiece. He has created us anew in Christ Jesus, so we can do the good things he planned for us long ago.

Ephesians 2:10 NLT

For Robert Simon it was the find of a lifetime! He discovered the masterpiece in an unlikely place—a Louisiana auction house. It was a gamble to pay $10,000 for the badly damaged oil-on-wood painting, but Simon saw something special in the piece, so he bought it.

It took six years of meticulous cleaning and restoration to remove centuries of dirt and overpaint from what most people regarded as a mere copy of Leonardo da Vinci's famous *Salvator Mundi*. Simon and his team brought in experts to run sophisticated tests to determine the age and authenticity of the work, the title of which means "Savior of the World."

Finally, the painting was brought before the world's leading da Vinci experts. Their verdict was unanimous: the painting was an original Leonardo da Vinci masterpiece! It sold at auction for $450.31 million. All because Robert Simon saw something special and pursued it.

God calls each one of us his masterpiece. Think about that! A masterpiece is an artist's greatest creation, a work carrying incredible value. When others view us, what do they see? When they witness our actions, are they drawn to find out more?

We've been remade—re-created by the Master's hand to reflect Jesus, our Savior. Notice that good works follow salvation in today's Bible text. There is nothing we can do to become a masterpiece on our own. It is purely through God's eternal grace and love that we are saved.

As we're remade more and more into Christ's likeness, good works follow. They are a testimony of what God has done for us in Jesus. Others are watching. They constantly observe and assess us. What do they see?

Sometimes we may be tempted to cover up our identity as children of God. We may hide our masterpiece selves behind our desire to fit in, to find acceptance by those around us. It's often too easy to join in the neighborhood gossip, to laugh at derogatory and debasing jokes, and otherwise try to reflect the world around us, instead of displaying our Master's treasure.

When we fail to reflect and display Christ through our actions, he forgives. The Holy Spirit renews our desire to perfectly display God's love, to show his inexplicable mercy and his unconditional forgiveness.

Jesus helps us demonstrate through every action our true identity as God's wonderfully made work of art!

𝒫𝓇𝒶𝓎𝑒𝓇 𝓈𝓉𝒶𝓇𝓉𝑒𝓇: Keep remaking me to better reflect you, Lord. Help me display your love through my actions every day, especially when . . .

Wonderful Witness

You are wonderfully made—made for love, for joy, for service. It's wonderful!

In all these ways and more, you get to share with those around you the Good News of the Savior. God has made you to . . .

Proclaim the excellencies of him who called you out of darkness into his marvelous light.

1 Peter 2:9

How wonderful!!

As you have walked with Jesus, what have you seen in him and learned from him?

How can you share these things with others?

O LORD, you have searched me and known me!
You know when I sit down and when I rise up;
    you discern my thoughts from afar.
You search out my path and my lying down
    and are acquainted with all my ways.
Even before a word is on my tongue,
    behold, O LORD, you know it altogether. . . .
Where shall I go from your Spirit?
    Or where shall I flee from your presence? . . .
If I take the wings of the morning
    and dwell in the uttermost parts of the sea,
even there your hand shall lead me,
    and your right hand shall hold me. . . .
For you formed my inward parts;
    you knitted me together in my mother's womb.
I praise you, for I am fearfully and wonderfully made.
Wonderful are your works;
    my soul knows it very well.
My frame was not hidden from you,
when I was being made in secret,
    intricately woven in the depths of the earth.
Your eyes saw my unformed substance;
in your book were written, every one of them,
    the days that were formed for me,
    when as yet there was none of them. . . .
Search me, O God, and know my heart!
    Try me and know my thoughts!
And see if there be any grievous way in me,
    and lead me in the way everlasting!

Psalm 139

To see all of CTA's devotion books and journals, visit us at www.CTAinc.com. You may order online or by calling 1-800-999-1874.

If this book has made a difference in your life or if you have simply enjoyed it, we would like to hear from you. Your words will encourage us!

Email: editor@CTAinc.com; include the subject line:
    WOGXXSC

Write: Editorial Manager, Department WOGXXSC
    CTA, Inc.
    PO Box 1205
    Fenton, MO 63026-1205

Comment online: www.CTAinc.com (search WOGXXSC)